HISTORY HUNTERS

TEMPLE

OF THE SUN

by Emma Thomas

Gareth Stevens Publishing
A WORLD ALMANAC EDUCATION GROUP COMPANY

Please visit our web site at: www.garethstevens.com
For a free color catalog describing Gareth Stevens Publishing's
list of high-quality books and multimedia programs,
call 1-800-542-2595 (USA) or 1-800-387-3178 (Canada).
Gareth Stevens Publishing's fax: (414) 332-3567.

Library of Congress Cataloging-in-Publication Data

Thomas, Emma.
    Temple of the Sun / by Emma Thomas. — North American ed.
        p. cm. — (History hunters)
    Summary: Describes a research expedition to study Incan textile fragments and other artifacts
in Peru.
    Includes bibliographical references and index.
    ISBN 0-8368-3744-4 (lib. bdg.)
    1. Incas—Peru—Cuzco Region—Antiquities—Juvenile literature.   2. Coricancha Temple Site (Cuzco, Peru)—
Juvenile literature.   3. Machu Picchu Site (Peru)—Juvenile literature.   4. Cuzco Region (Peru)—Antiquities—
Juvenile literature.   [1. Incas—Antiquities.   2. Coricancha Temple Site (Cuzco, Peru).   3. Machu Picchu Site
(Peru).   4. Indians of South America—Antiquities.   5. Peru—Antiquities.   6. Archaeology.]   I. Title.
II. Series.
    F3429.T273   2003
    746'.089'9832308537—dc21   2003045741

This North American edition first published in 2004 by
Gareth Stevens Publishing
A World Almanac Education Group Company
330 West Olive Street, Suite 100
Milwaukee, WI 53212 USA

We would like to thank: Nick Owen, Dr. Colin McEwan at The British Museum, Elizabeth Wiggans and the
people of the Patacancha Valley, Peru.

Gareth Stevens editor: Carol Ryback
Gareth Stevens cover design: Katherine A. Goedheer

Photo credits:
t=top, b=bottom, c=center, l=left, r=right, OFC=outside front cover, OBC=outside back cover
Alamy: 3br, 3bl, 5tc, 7c, 14-15, 14bl, 17tr, 17cr, 21tr, 22-23, 28-29. Adriana von Hagen: 25c, 28tr.
Corbis: 6br, 7cr, 7br, 9tr, 10tr, 12-13, 12tr, 13br, 15br, 20-21. David Drew: 8tr, 11cr, 11br, 12br,
15tr, 15cr, 18tr, 18br, 19tl, 19cr, 19cl, 20tr, 21br, 22br, 23cr, 23br, 23bl, 24cr, 24bl. Dumbarton
Oaks, Washington, DC: 4br. National Geographic Image Collection, Washington, DC: 14br, 15bl.
Natural History Museum: 20bl. Werner Forman Archive (British Museum): 5tl.

Every effort has been made to trace the copyright holders, and we apologize in advance for any
unintentional omissions. We would be pleased to insert the appropriate acknowledgments in any
subsequent edition of this publication.

Printed in Hong Kong

1 2 3 4 5 6 7 8 9 07 06 05 04 03

Would you like to join an exciting expedition to Peru?
The characters accompanying you — Dr. McLeish, Sam Owen and Dr. Orellana — are fictitious, but the facts about historians and archaeologists represent an accurate view of their work. The highland village of Yanacocha and the mummy found there are also fictitious, but the characteristics of the mummy and details about life in the highlands of Peru are based on fact.

Can't wait to learn more? Ready to go exploring?

Then welcome to the City Museum...

CONTENTS

CITY MUSEUM PASS

Name: Dr. Elizabeth McLeish
Position: Curator
Department: Ancient Americas

Interests: History, exploring, and hiking.

CITY MUSEUM PASS

Name: Sam Owen
Position: Research Assistant
Department: Ancient Americas

Interests: History, computers, and football.

TEMPORARY

Day 1

I'm spending my vacation helping Dr. Liz McLeish, who is the curator, or head, of the Ancient Americas department at the City Museum. All of the artifacts in the Ancient Americas gallery are a bequest by Sir Cedric Barking, a Victorian-era explorer. (When someone dies and leaves items to someone or some organization in a will, it is called a bequest. Many museums obtain rare and valuable items thanks to bequethals.)

Sir Cedric visited Peru, South America, many times to study the history of the Incan people. Dr. McLeish completed the research for her Ph.D. in Peru.

This afternoon, we met with Sir Cedric's grandson, Sir Dennis Barking. He gave the museum some more artifacts from the Barking family archive — a wooden goblet, a mysterious old letter, and a fragment of woven cloth. Dr. McLeish is very excited about these additions. She is certain they are Incan!

Cuzco, Peru, August 18, 1887

Dear Sir Cedric,

Do you remember me telling you about the people of Yanacocha in the highlands? I enclose a fragment from an ancient, beautiful Yanacocha textile. I have never seen anything like it. Along with the textile, I am sending a wooden cup. Could you please tell me your expert opinion regarding these items?

By the way, Mr. Mallendar has been helping me with my English. He says I am doing very well. What do you think?

Tu gran amigo,

Padre Luis

Summer 1999
My good friends from Peru pose with one of their alpacas.

Our textile's design is similar to this very famous Incan artifact — the "All-T'oqapu Tunic." The tunic is made from one piece of cloth, with openings for the arms and head.

This goblet, called a **kero** in the Quechua language of the Inca, was used for drinking beer during special rituals or celebrations. Quechua is still spoken in Peru.

WHO WERE THE INCA?
by Sir Cedric Barking

For fifty years I have studied the fascinating people called the Inca. We believe their distant ancestors were Stone Age hunters who crossed to North America from Asia more than 12,000 years ago. Over time, these hunters moved south into what is now South America, where they became farmers.

In A.D. 1400, the Inca were simply a tribe of highland farmers. Over the course of the next one hundred years, through diplomacy and war, the Inca took control of thousands of miles of territory. They ruled about ten million people and eventually built the greatest empire the region had ever seen.

Scholar and explorer Sir Cedric Barking on his first expedition to Peru.

The textile fragment is made of alpaca wool. Alpacas are like llamas but with thicker, softer fleece.

From: Dr. Jorge Orellana, The University, Cuzco, Peru
To: Dr. Liz McLeish, The City Museum
Subject: Exciting Incan artifacts

Dear Liz,
It was wonderful to hear from you. Thanks for e-mailing me the images of the artifacts. The textile pattern is definitely Incan. The *kero* is very interesting, too. Stories, myths, and history were often painted on *keros*. For example, this design shows two jungle warriors wearing elaborate headdresses. Sometimes these goblets were made in pairs — could there be a mate to it somewhere? I also believe the textile is of extreme importance and warrants further investigation. Can you travel to Peru for some research this year? Anytime between May and the beginning of our rainy season in October would work best. It will be great to see you again.
¡Hasta pronto!
Regards, Jorge.

USER 1
USER 2
USER 3

Day 10

I could hardly believe it when Dr. McLeish said that I could accompany her on a research trip to Peru. The Barking family decided to pay for the expedition — so we are on our way!

South America is a huge continent with thirteen independent countries. Peru lies on the western coast, and it is just a little smaller than Texas, New Mexico, and Arizona combined. The territory that the Inca controlled extended beyond Peru, stretching almost 3,000 miles (4,828 kilometers) from north to south. Their empire was rich in gold, silver, and other minerals. Before the Inca, other civilizations lived along the Pacific coast. Rich natural resources from the sea to the fertile valleys made Peru an ideal place to settle.

We are flying south from Lima, the capital of Peru, into the Andes, the mountain chain that runs the length of South America. We will land in Cuzco, the capital of the Inca.

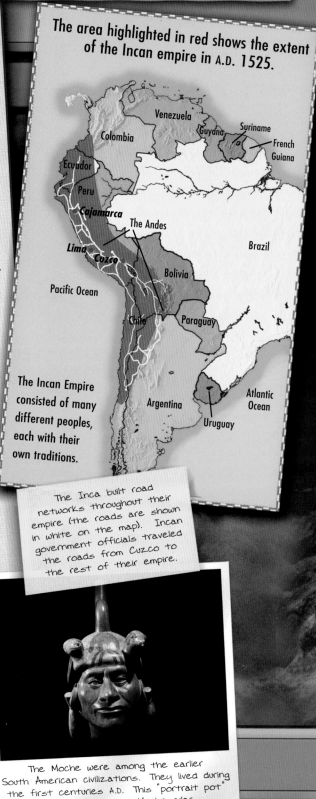

The area highlighted in red shows the extent of the Incan empire in A.D. 1525.

The Incan Empire consisted of many different peoples, each with their own traditions.

The Inca built road networks throughout their empire (the roads are shown in white on the map). Incan government officials traveled the roads from Cuzco to the rest of their empire.

The Moche were among the earlier South American civilizations. They lived during the first centuries A.D. This "portrait pot" probably depicts a Moche ruler.

THE STORY OF THE CONQUISTADORES

The Andes is the longest mountain range in the world.

Dr. McLeish has given me a fascinating book about the destruction of the Incan Empire. She says it's important for me to understand what happened to the Inca if I am going to help with historical research in Peru.

I n 1532, a Spanish adventurer, Francisco Pizarro, and his band of 168 "Conquistadores" landed in northern Peru. They had come from Spain in search of riches. When they arrived, a civil war was raging between two branches of the Incan royal family.

One side was led by the Incan ruler Atahualpa. He agreed to meet for negotiations with Pizarro and his men at the Incan town of Cajamarca. The Spaniards tricked Atahualpa and held him hostage. Atahualpa's followers collected an enormous ransom of gold and silver, but the Spaniards took the treasure and ruthlessly murdered the Incan leader.

The statue shows Francisco Pizarro on horseback. Spaniards brought horses to South America, including Peru.

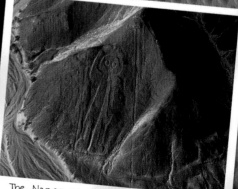

The Nazca people lived on the western desert coast in the first centuries A.D. They created the "Nazca Lines" – enormous, mysterious drawings on the landscape.

AN INCAN MUMMY

Day 11

The altitude in Cuzco is over 11,000 feet (3,400 meters) above sea level. The air is thin up here, and I felt dizzy and a little sick at first. I wanted to lie down for a few hours, but Dr. McLeish insisted that we go straight to Dr. Orellana's office. He made us some coca leaf tea to help us acclimatize, or adjust to the altitude.

Dr. Orellana believes our textile was cut from a larger garment. It was probably made for a male member of the Incan royal family. Incrustations and small stains on the fabric make Dr. Orellana think that the tunic might have been used to wrap an Incan mummy! I asked Dr. Orellana if we might still find the mummy somewhere. Dr. McLeish said that because the textile originally came from the highlands, where the climate is very damp, chances are that the mummy has deteriorated. Then Dr. Orellana smiled and handed us an interesting magazine article — he thinks we might find the mummy after all!

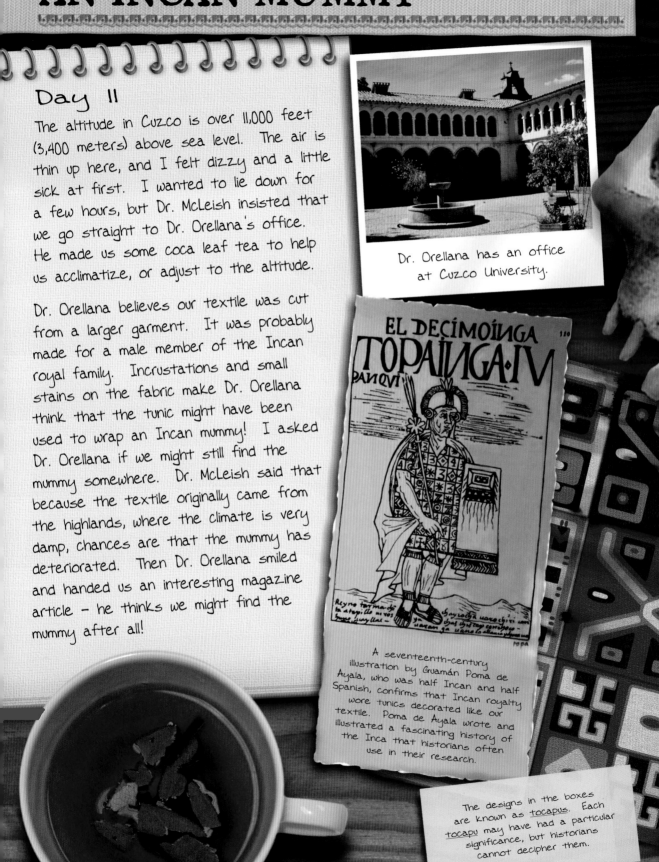

Dr. Orellana has an office at Cuzco University.

EL DECÍMOINGA TOPAINGA·IV PANQVI

A seventeenth-century illustration by Guamán Poma de Ayala, who was half Incan and half Spanish, confirms that Incan royalty wore tunics decorated like our textile. Poma de Ayala wrote and illustrated a fascinating history of the Inca that historians often use in their research.

The designs in the boxes are known as tocapus. Each tocapu may have had a particular significance, but historians cannot decipher them.

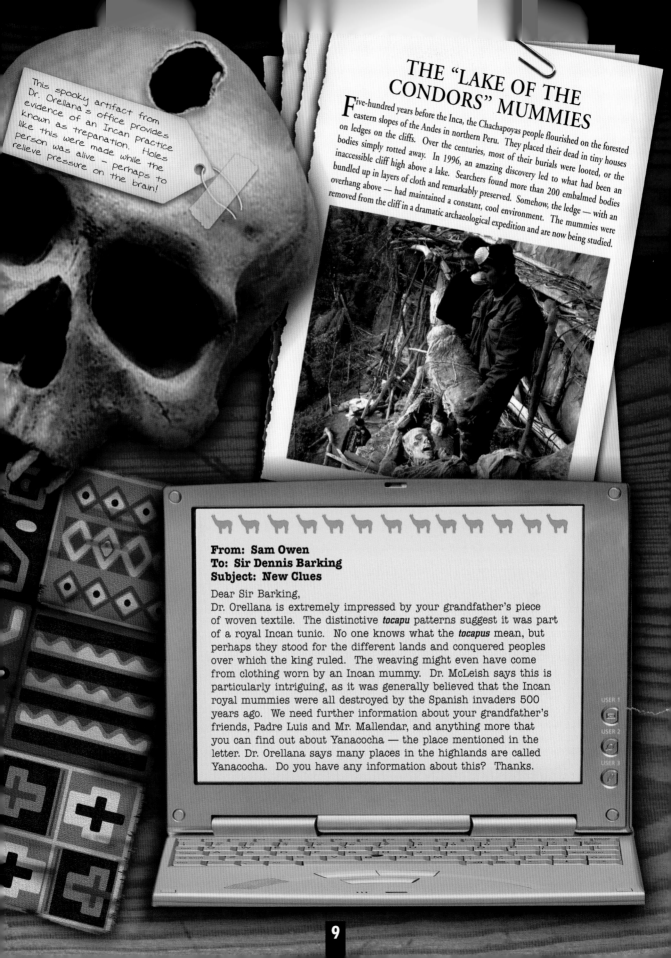

This spooky artifact from Dr. Orellana's office provides evidence of an Incan practice known as trepanation. Holes like this were made while the person was alive — perhaps to relieve pressure on the brain!

THE "LAKE OF THE CONDORS" MUMMIES

Five-hundred years before the Inca, the Chachapoyas people flourished on the forested eastern slopes of the Andes in northern Peru. They placed their dead in tiny houses on ledges on the cliffs. Over the centuries, most of their burials were looted, or the bodies simply rotted away. In 1996, an amazing discovery led to what had been an inaccessible cliff high above a lake. Searchers found more than 200 embalmed bodies bundled up in layers of cloth and remarkably preserved. Somehow, the ledge — with an overhang above — had maintained a constant, cool environment. The mummies were removed from the cliff in a dramatic archaeological expedition and are now being studied.

From: Sam Owen
To: Sir Dennis Barking
Subject: New Clues

Dear Sir Barking,

Dr. Orellana is extremely impressed by your grandfather's piece of woven textile. The distinctive *tocapu* patterns suggest it was part of a royal Incan tunic. No one knows what the *tocapus* mean, but perhaps they stood for the different lands and conquered peoples over which the king ruled. The weaving might even have come from clothing worn by an Incan mummy. Dr. McLeish says this is particularly intriguing, as it was generally believed that the Incan royal mummies were all destroyed by the Spanish invaders 500 years ago. We need further information about your grandfather's friends, Padre Luis and Mr. Mallendar, and anything more that you can find out about Yanacocha — the place mentioned in the letter. Dr. Orellana says many places in the highlands are called Yanacocha. Do you have any information about this? Thanks.

USER 1
USER 2
USER 3

THE INCAN CAPITAL

Day 12

I woke up full of energy, but the air still feels thin, and walking uphill is a struggle. While Dr. McLeish and Dr. Orellana met with some research students, I took a walk around Cuzco, the holy center of the Incan world.

In Incan times, Cuzco's main square was surrounded by palaces. Dr. McLeish says that when an Incan king died, his palace became a sacred place. The deceased ruler was not mummified in the same way ancient Egyptian rulers were. Instead, he was embalmed and kept in his palace. Close relatives looked after him as if he were still alive, worshipping him as a godlike ancestor. Royal mummies were fed, clothed, and regularly paraded around the city. They even took part in important ceremonies!

Incan stonework is everywhere in Cuzco. Today, many Incan palace walls still support parts of modern buildings.

Dear Mom and Dad,

This afternoon we visited Sacsahuaman, a sacred Incan site and fortress on the outskirts of Cuzco. Sacsahuaman is a fantastic example of Incan stonemasonry. I'm becoming an expert on South American mummies and the Inca. This postcard shows a 2,000-year-old mummy from the Peruvian coast. It was remarkably preserved by the dry desert conditions. I'm hoping that I get to see an actual Incan mummy before we leave Peru.

A royal Incan mummy is carried aloft in a procession.

The Sacsahuaman fortress was built with massive blocks that fit together so perfectly no mortar was used. Each block weighed up to 100 tons (91 tonnes). Historians believe it took 30,000 people about 30 years to build Sacsahuaman.

THE STORY OF THE CONQUISTADORES

After Atahualpa's murder, his enemies became Pizarro's allies. The Spanish Conquistadores laid seige to Cuzco, and a young prince called Manco became the Incan king, with Spanish support, in December 1533. But Pizarro and his Conquistadores eventually betrayed Manco, too. They ransacked the empire and took control. The Incan people were abused and their treasures plundered.

More and more invaders were coming from Spain. Manco realized that the Incan empire was on the brink of destruction. He secretly fled Cuzco to gather his forces and returned to battle for control of the city. Manco's army almost succeeded, but Spanish reinforcements arrived just in time to defeat the Inca.

The Conquistadores stripped and melted down the gold and silver that decorated the holiest Incan temple — the original Temple of the Sun — in Cuzco.

This gold and silver maize cob is from the temple's artificial garden. All the plants in the garden were made from precious metals.

The curved wall of the original Temple of the Sun was incorporated into the colonial church of Santo Domingo.

Cuzco City Plan

Cuzco was built under the direction of Pachacuti, the greatest of all the Incan rulers. It was laid out in the shape of a puma — an animal sacred to the Inca.

Sacsahuaman

The central square

The Temple of the Sun

Day 15

What an incredible trip. I thought I'd spend hours digging up old ruins, but studying history in Peru isn't like that at all – the history of the Inca is all around us. Dr. McLeish and I are in the Incan town of Ollantaytambo. It was built on the Urubamba River, in an area that is known as the "Sacred Valley of the Inca."

Dr. McLeish worked here for many years and helped the community set up a small museum. The museum has displays on the history of Ollantaytambo, and it highlights many of the Incan traditions maintained by the local people today.

From town, you can see giant steps going up the mountainside. Dr. McLeish tells me that these "agricultural terraces" with their stone retaining walls were built by the Inca. The terraces protect against soil erosion, providing flat land for growing food. The main crop grown in the valley was, and still is, maize – the sacred crop of the Inca.

Dr. McLeish's friends from Ollantaytambo drink some <u>chicha</u> (maize beer). People from older cultures drank beer from wooden <u>keros</u>.

Maize cobs dry in the sun. What isn't sold will be kept for cooking or making beer.

Maize was a versatile crop. It was boiled, roasted, eaten on the cob, or ground up to make flour.

THE STORY OF THE CONQUISTADORES

After their defeat at Cuzco, Manco and his army retreated and occupied the town of Ollantaytambo. They strengthened the town with extra walls and fortifications, resisted a Spanish attack, and inflicted a rare defeat on the Spanish invaders. But Manco knew that he was vulnerable in Ollantaytambo. He retreated to a place where the Spaniards couldn't find him.

According to Incan history, Manco left Ollantaytambo in 1537 for Vilcabamba, a remote region of mountains and jungle. He was probably accompanied by his wives, sons, herds of llamas and alpacas, thousands of his followers, and the mummies of his royal ancestors.

Residents of Ollantaytambo wear a mixture of traditional and modern clothing.

From: **Dr. Jorge Orellana, The University, Cuzco, Peru**
To: **Sam Owen**
Subject: **Pachacuti — the first great Incan ruler**

Dear Liz and Sam,

¡Hola! Here's an interesting development — I have a hunch that Pachacuti, the first great Incan ruler, is somehow linked to your textile. As you know, he built the town at Ollantaytambo and helped establish many other places in that region. Some old Spanish documents are becoming increasingly important in our attempts to piece together what we can of Incan history, and I am going to spend a little more time in the Cuzco archives. I will explain more when I catch up with you tomorrow.

P.S. Ollantaytambo makes the best *chicha* in all of Peru. Don't you agree?

MACHU PICCHU

Day 18

I could barely wait to see the most famous Incan city of them all – Machu Picchu. Surrounded by mountain peaks and jungle, Machu Picchu's buildings remain in extraordinary condition. Little has changed since the time of the Inca – only the thatched roofs are missing.

No road leads to Machu Picchu, so we caught the train. Beyond Ollantaytambo, the landscape changes rapidly, and within an hour, we were in a completely different environment – a hot, sticky jungle with orchids and butterflies.

Less than one hundred years ago, American explorer Hiram Bingham revealed Machu Picchu to the rest of the world. When he arrived in 1911, most of the ruins were hidden under thick forest. Bingham thought he had discovered the original capital city of the Inca. Machu Picchu means "bigger peak," while the nearby mountain, named Huayna Picch, means "smaller peak."

The Inca believed mountains were sacred places inhabited by powerful spirits. Machu Picchu provides glorious views of mountain peaks on every side.

The Discovery of machu Picchu

In 1911, Hiram Bingham was traveling around Peru looking for Incan ruins. no one outside of Peru knew about machu Picchu. Then – outside of Ollantaytambo – Bingham met a farmer who was clearing the jungle to plant crops.

Bingham asked the farmer if there were any interesting ruins in the area. The farmer told him about some Incan buildings on top of the nearby mountain.

The train to Machu Picchu follows the Urubamba River.

The Torreon, a curved granite altar used for solar worship, includes a window oriented to the biannual solstice sunrises.

A natural cave lined with carved stone sits beneath the Sun temple. Archaeologists think that mummies were stored inside large niches cut into the rock.

The farmer and a local boy guided Bingham up the jungle-covered hillside to Machu Picchu. It has 200 remarkably preserved Incan buildings with extraordinary stonework. Local people always knew about the ruins, but archaeologists consider Bingham the "discoverer" of Machu Picchu. It is one of the most famous discoveries in the history of twentieth-century archaeology.

Camp Machu Picchu

Dr. Orellana arrived at our camp this evening with a map of the area. His investigations in Cuzco were successful, and he had uncovered some exciting information. The Spanish records state that Manco and most of his followers settled further west in the Vilcabamba region – not at Machu Picchu as Hiram Bingham believed. In fact, Machu Picchu isn't mentioned anywhere in the Spaniards' records, and no one knows what was occurring in Machu Picchu at the time of the Conquest.

Dr. Orellana said other documents in the Cuzco archives from 1568 listed the lands of "Picho" as part of the personal estate of the Incan King Pachacuti – who also owned another small palace to the north of Machu Picchu, called Guamán Marca.

Then Dr. Orellana pointed to the map. In the unexplored mountains between the two royal estates, he marked a cross and wrote . . . Yanacocha!

The Urubamba Valley was one of the first regions to be conquered by the great Pachacuti, during the earliest phase of Inca empire-building. After his death, his immediate family continued looking after his palaces and country estates. A new ruler would have built his own properties.

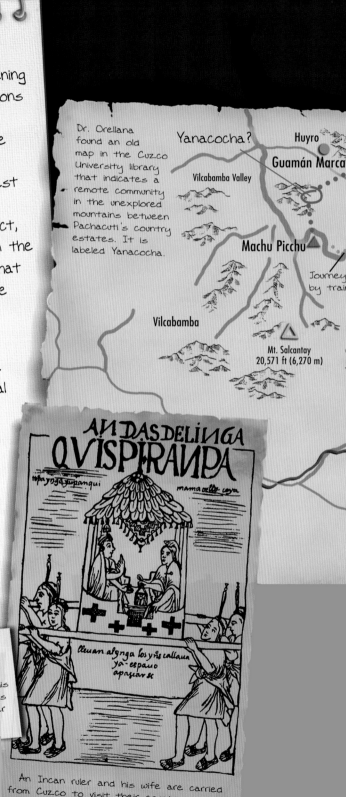

Dr. Orellana found an old map in the Cuzco University library that indicates a remote community in the unexplored mountains between Pachacuti's country estates. It is labeled Yanacocha.

Yanacocha?

Huyro

Guamán Marca

Vilcabamba Valley

Machu Picchu

Journey by train

Vilcabamba

Mt. Salcantay
20,571 ft (6,270 m)

AN DAS DELINGA QVISPIRAPA

topa ynga yupanqui

mama ocllo coya

lleuan algnga los yris callana ya-espano apascarse

An Incan ruler and his wife are carried from Cuzco to visit their country estates.

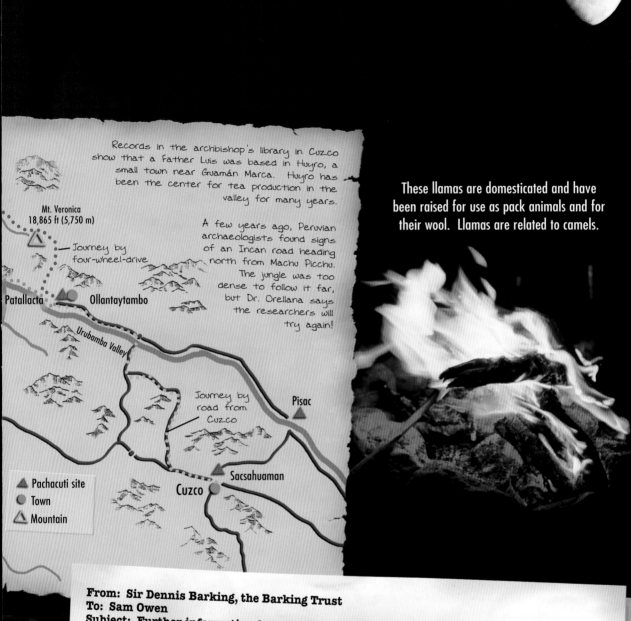

Records in the archbishop's library in Cuzco show that a Father Luis was based in Huyro, a small town near Guamán Marca. Huyro has been the center for tea production in the valley for many years.

A few years ago, Peruvian archaeologists found signs of an Incan road heading north from Machu Picchu. The jungle was too dense to follow it far, but Dr. Orellana says the researchers will try again!

Mt. Veronica
18,865 ft (5,750 m)

Journey by four-wheel-drive

Patallacta

Ollantaytambo

Urubamba Valley

Journey by road from Cuzco

Pisac

Sacsahuaman

Cuzco

▲ Pachacuti site
● Town
△ Mountain

These llamas are domesticated and have been raised for use as pack animals and for their wool. Llamas are related to camels.

From: Sir Dennis Barking, the Barking Trust
To: Sam Owen
Subject: Further information from the Barking archives

Dear Sam and Liz,
We found a letter dated September 25, 1887, in the Barking family archives from Mr. Edward Mallendar, "The Plantation," Huyro, Peru. Mr. Mallendar wants to inform Sir Cedric of the death of his friend, Father Luis, earlier that month. Does this help in any way with your search?

From: Sam Owen
To: Sir Dennis Barking, The Barking Trust

Your information certainly does help. Earlier today, Dr. Orellana located a place called Yanacocha in the hills between Machu Picchu and an Incan site called Guamán Marca. And guess what – there is a town called Huyro nearby. A team of local archaeologists will soon embark on an expedition to follow an unexplored Incan road from Machu Picchu toward Guamán Marca. We will also lead a second expedition in the opposite direction. We will hope to find Yanacocha along the way!

A ROYAL VILLAGE

Day 19

After a bumpy ride in an old four-wheel-drive vehicle, we arrived in the village of Guamán Marca. While Señor Rosas, our mule handler and guide, made preparations for the expedition, we explored the remains of "Pachacuti's palace." Compared to Machu Picchu, Guamán Marca is small, simple, and sort of run-down. The palace was built on a flattened piece of land. It originally had four sets of buildings surrounding an inner courtyard or patio — somewhat like a Roman villa. The central courtyard is now the village soccer field! Like Machu Picchu, this site above the Lucomayo River offers incredible views up and down the valley. Pachacuti and his advisers chose a magnificent natural setting for their architecture.

Señor Rosas told us to get to bed early. We will be leaving at first light and could be on the trail for two days.

Children pose in the ruins of a palace doorway. The high-quality stonework of granite blocks is typical of the architecture of Pachacuti. The site's official guardian, a local man, encourages the children to help look after the ruins and keep it free of vegetation — after all, not every village possesses an Incan palace.

mas de treinta años que la dicha Guaman Marca nunca fue sembrada ni cultivada de ningunas chacaras de coca ni de maíz mas de que las dichas tierras fueron de Ynga Yupanqui que tenia alli para su recreacion por no entrar dentro del valle

Luckily for historians, the sixteenth-century Spaniards kept detailed records. Dr. Orellana translated this 1579 document of their interviews with the local people. It confirms that the Guamán Marca lands originally belonged to "Ynga [Inca] Yupanqui [another name for Pachacuti] para su recreacion [for his recreation]." Dr. Orellana was right when he called Guamán Marca one of Pachacuti's country estates!

We pitched our tents on the central courtyard. Any archaeological evidence that once existed here was destroyed long ago. The courtyard has been cultivated and has served as the village soccer field for many years.

Señor Rosas cooked us a delicious supper of fried yuca, or cassava (a root vegetable). Yuca grows on lower mountain slopes.

Señor Rosas's men make sure the animals are well shod for our journey. The Inca used llamas as their beasts of burden. Spaniards introduced horses and mules, which can carry much bigger loads, to the area.

We must evenly distribute our loads of tents and food on the pack animals. Stubborn mules often refuse to move if they feel uncomfortable.

We did some last-minute shopping in Huyro. Merchants display their wares, including herbs, spices, and dyes for the local weavers, on the ground instead of in shops.

I bought a Peruvian hat and gloves. Dr. McLeish says that traditional designs have been adapted for tourists and are exported around the world.

Day 21

We hit some nasty weather. Down in the jungle, we sloshed through deep mud that made it nearly impossible to get through the dense undergrowth. But despite the miserable conditions, it's been interesting.

This morning, Dr. McLeish signaled for us to be quiet — we came upon a young Andean bear, or "spectacled bear," foraging in front of us. Dr. Orellana explained that at one time, these bears were freely hunted in this region. Now, they are protected by international law.

Later, as we cleared a section of Incan road to take a photograph, I noticed a small snake staring at me. Señor Rosas leaped forward and cut off its head with his machete! I was pretty shocked, but Dr. Orellana said it was a deadly coral snake. Señor Rosas put the snake head in his pocket. He plans to keep it in the loft of his house as a good luck charm. From now on, I'm wearing my thickest socks, and I am going to keep my pant legs tucked into them.

This Incan road running through the jungle is very well built. Some sections even have steps.

The Inca built roads through jungle, across deserts, and over mountains to link all the diverse environments of their empire. Special state messengers called <u>chasquis</u> ran in relays to send important messages between Incan cities.

The spectacled bear is South America's only bear. It gets its name from the pale patches around its eyes. Spectacled bears are timid and very rarely seen. They eat fruits, leaves, roots, and small animals, such as rabbits, birds, and mice.

When the jungle started to thin out, the trail got easier. We climbed until dusk, when we noticed the distant shapes of houses and began to hear ferocious barking. We have found Yanacocha! I'm too tired to write more.

Houses in Yanacocha have thatched roofs and walls of mud brick and plaster. Incan houses built six hundred years ago would have been made of the same stuff!

Day 22

We awoke at first light. Yanacocha is not so much a real village as scattered groups of houses. Dr. McLeish says extended families – perhaps three generations living together – occupy each dwelling. All the family members look after the children and animals, and all share the work on the land. It's a hard life up here – the altitude is about 11,800 feet (3,600 m).

We split into two groups to explore the area. The villagers dress in traditional garments. Men wear brightly colored ponchos. Women wear mantles, or carrying cloths, in which they wrap their babies. We saw many women weaving. The Inca valued beautiful textiles more highly than the finest works of gold or silver – something the Spanish invaders (the Conquistadores) found impossible to understand!

We noticed that the villagers' woven designs closely resemble the <u>tocapus</u> on our swatch of the Barking textile.

Maize will not grow at this altitude. Instead, the principal crop is potatoes.

Potatoes are native to the Andes region. About 200 different varieties of potatoes grow here.

Like the Inca, people of Yanacocha are llama herders. Llamas are used as pack animals. Villagers often travel to the valley to exchange potatoes for products such as maize.

A group of women weave fabric on looms similar to those used by their ancestors. Textiles and weavings played an important role in Incan culture and art.

This small, well-built Incan building was probably a <u>tambo</u>, or wayside, for official Incan travelers. It's proof that we're following an important Incan route!

No one in the village could find the key to this tiny, locked church. I found that strange . . .

TEMPLE OF THE SUN

Day 23

Members of the Peruvian archeological team arrived last night from Machu Picchu. They uncovered the other half of the Incan road and followed it through the jungle to Yanacocha.

Dr. Orellana is a native Peruvian, so the Yanacocha villagers agreed to meet with us. We asked about other ruins in the vicinity. After talking among themselves for a while, their mayor said they had something we might want to see. We walked for about twenty minutes until we reached a rocky outcrop above a lake. The villagers led us up to a narrow cave entrance that was invisible from below.

As we peered inside, an early morning sunbeam highlighted a carved niche holding a mummy! Dr. Orellana said, "I've never seen anything like this before. It's like a small, lonely 'Temple of the Sun.'"

One of the Peruvian archaeologists met with the community council. The council consists of members from the main families living in the village.

The mummy enjoyed a great view looking straight east. The Sun rises almost directly behind the snowy peak of Mount Veronica.

We found the mummy in a flexed position with its hands folded across its body. Most of the original wrappings were gone.

Natural rock steps led to the cave, which was lined with cut granite blocks.

Burnt offerings and pieces of broken pots littered the ground. A wooden *kero* — the twin to the one in the Barking collection — lay nearby!

From: Sam Owen
To: Sir Dennis Barking, the Barking Trust
Subject: The end of our quest?

Dear Sir Dennis,
You will never guess what happened next! As we left the cave, Dr. Orellana spoke in Quechua to the mayor. He asked if the mummy had ever been wrapped in anything else. The mayor began to smile and motioned for us to follow him once more. He led us to the locked chapel we had seen the day before, pulled out a key he kept hidden in a small woven bag, and opened the door. The plain interior contained nothing but a simple altar and a statue of the Christ child. The mayor dragged a carved wooden box from beneath the altar. He lifted the lid and removed a brightly colored weaving. It was a man's tunic — with a square section missing! The mayor explained that long ago the mummy had been wrapped in the tunic, but when the church was built, the textile was removed from the cave and stored here under the altar. His grandparents told him that when they were young, a priest from the valley had cut off a piece of the garment and taken it away. Since then, the chapel was kept locked. I think that young priest was Padre Luis!

One week later

This morning, we met in Dr. Orellana's office to piece together the information we gathered on our trip. I felt like part of a team of history detectives. Dr. Orellana stressed that his ideas were only theories, but I found the story fascinating.

Machu Picchu, the private estate of the great Inca Pachacuti, would have been maintained by Pachacuti's family from his death in 1490 until the Spanish Conquest. When Manco fled into the nearby region of Vilcabamba with many of the royal mummies from Cuzco, members of Pachacuti's family probably decided to retrieve some of their important mummified ancestors as well. As the Conquistadores moved closer to Machu Picchu, Pachacuti's family removed the mummy they valued most and took it up the Incan road to Yanacocha — a remote place where it might be kept in safety. Machu Picchu was abandoned and quickly engulfed by the jungle.

Although the Spaniards destroyed many other cities, they never reached Machu Picchu.

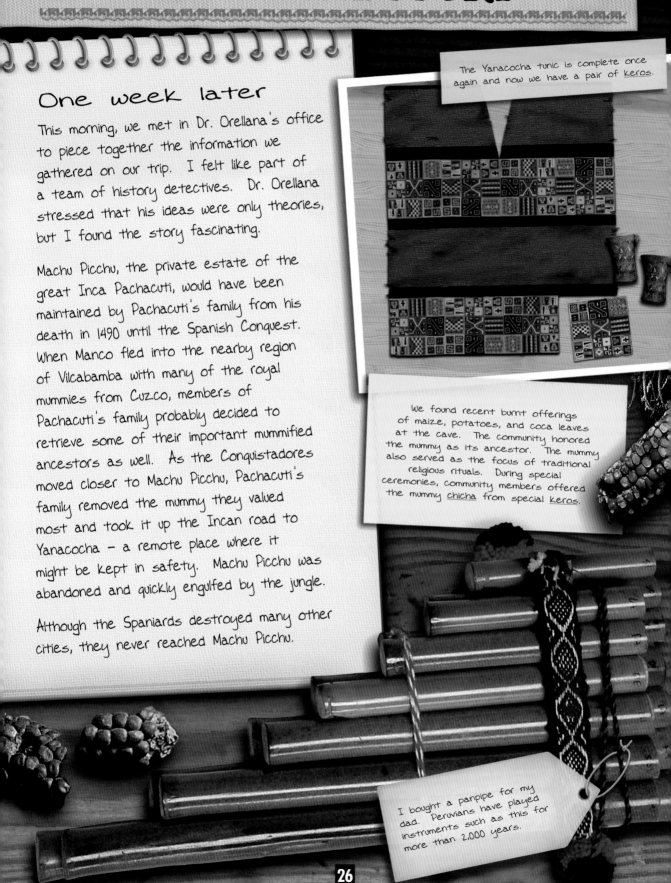

The Yanacocha tunic is complete once again and now we have a pair of <u>keros</u>.

We found recent burnt offerings of maize, potatoes, and coca leaves at the cave. The community honored the mummy as its ancestor. The mummy also served as the focus of traditional religious rituals. During special ceremonies, community members offered the mummy <u>chicha</u> from special <u>keros</u>.

I bought a panpipe for my dad. Peruvians have played instruments such as this for more than 2,000 years.

THE STORY OF THE CONQUISTADORES

Inca Manco, his wives, his sons, and their followers lived in exile for nearly forty years. In 1572, the Spaniards invaded Vilcabamba and executed the last of the Inca rulers, Tupac Amaru, Manco's youngest son.

The Conquest had devastating effects. Millions of people died, while others were forced to leave their homes to work for the invaders in mines or on farms. But high in the mountains, small communities lived quietly. For hundreds of years, their traditions and simple ways survived.

The Inca people had no written language. Instead, they kept records using knotted and colored strings called quipus (KEY pooz). Knot position and number, as well as the colors used, could have served as a calendar or indicated astronomical positions. Some historians believe quipus also functioned as coded mnemonic (memory) devices for transmitting information, history, or legends.

From: Sam Owen
To: Sir Dennis Barking, the Barking Trust
Subject: The story of the Yanacocha mummy

Dear Sir Dennis,
We think we've solved the mystery of the textile. Padre Luis occasionally performed mass in the church at Yanacocha. He was probably the one who snipped off the swatch of the tunic and somehow obtained the wooden *kero*. Padre Luis knew nothing of the cave. Its existence was kept a closely guarded secret until now. Why now? Dr. Orellana guesses that the villagers have long forgotten their reasons for protecting the mummy in the cave. They are tired of living in fear of looters who might steal the mummy or destroy their village in search of perceived treasures. When the villagers saw the little museum in Ollantaytambo, they decided it was time to let the mummy go. Now others can share the knowledge of and mystery behind the mummy, its tunic, and the keros, and the responsibility of keeping them safe for eternity.

The Inca extended their weaving skills to include bridges of braided rope that spanned Andean rivers. Today, only one community in Peru makes woven bridges.

PEOPLE OF THE ANDES

A grand opening

Tonight was the official opening of the City Museum's new "Barking Gallery." The new gallery is dedicated to the ancient and modern people of the Andes. Sir Cedric's collection is on display along with material from our recent Peruvian expedition. Special guests at the gala included villagers who traveled all the way from Yanacocha. The highlight of the evening was their presentation of a replica tunic to Sir Dennis and Dr. McLeish.

My extraordinary adventure with these Peruvian artifacts serves as a fantastic illustration of an important learning experience: The study of the past is more than just digging things up or reviewing old documents. Traditional societies, like the one we visited in highland Peru, give us insight into the culture and history of life in ancient times. We have much to learn from them about the mysteries of the past.

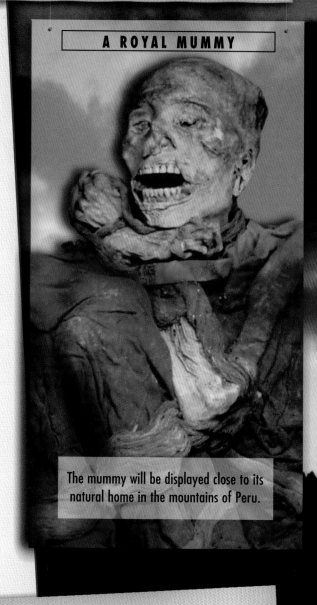

A ROYAL MUMMY

The mummy will be displayed close to its natural home in the mountains of Peru.

Dear Liz, Will, and Sir Dennis,

Thank you, my friends, for leaving the tunic in Cuzco and for returning the kero. I am sad that I had to miss the gallery's grand opening, but I had an important meeting here in Peru. The good news is that we secured funding to display the mummy and the other artifacts close to where they originated. Chemical analyses linked the hair and other residue from the tunic to the mummy, and now we believe it is in fact a royal Incan mummy. But we may never know its exact identity. Perhaps it is a lesser Incan prince, or — as some researchers suggested — the embalmed Inca Pachacuti himself. While I enjoy speculation, I also must not jump to conclusions. I must study many more artifacts in order to answer all our questions. For now, I send my best wishes and thanks to all. Please return to our beautiful country someday — perhaps for the opening of our new gallery? Jorge Orellana

THE REPLICA TUNIC

TRADITIONAL WEAVING

The people of Yanacocha created a beautiful replica tunic for the City Museum, using traditional weaving techniques and fine alpaca wool.

The Barking Trust has officially returned the *kero* and textile fragment to Peru. The original tunic has now been reunited with its missing piece.

LEGACY OF THE PAST

Clothing styles and music may change slightly with each generation, but cultural traditions endure.

GLOSSARY

acclimatize: to adapt to a new climate or altitude.

alpacas: domesticated animals raised in Peru for their thick wool. Alpacas are related to llamas.

altitude: the height of a place above sea level.

ancestors: relatives from whom you are descended.

archaeologists: scientists who study the past by examining the physical remains left behind.

archives: collections of historical documents and records.

artifacts: objects made by humans, such as tools, weavings, or pottery, that are often used for archeological study of past cultures.

Atahualpa: the Inca leader taken hostage, held for ransom, and murdered by Francisco Pizzaro in 1532.

biannual: occurring twice in one year.

chasquis: relay runners who carried important messages and lightweight packages between Incan cities.

chicha: beer made from maize.

civil war: a war between two groups of people from the same country.

coca leaf tea: tea made from the leaves of the coca bush.

Conquest: the period during the sixteenth century when Spaniards captured South American territories.

Conquistadores: the sixteenth-century Spanish conquerors of South America.

conservation: the scientific process of cleaning, mending, and preserving something.

curator: a staff member of a museum in charge of a collection.

diplomacy: a way of dealing with people carefully, tactfully, and in as fair a manner as possible.

embalmed: having undergone a chemical treatment that helps prevent decay of a dead body.

erosion: the process of wearing away by wind, water, weather, or contact with some other foreign object.

estate: a large property with an enormous house, often located far from a city. Estates are usually tended by indoor servants and outdoor groundskeepers.

fieldwork: practical experience that takes place away from a traditional classroom and that helps students gain a better understanding of a subject.

fleece: a soft or woolly covering of an animal, such as sheep, llamas, or alpacas.

fragment: an incomplete portion of an object.

granite: a very hard type of igneous, or volcanic, rock often used for buildings or monuments.

inaccessible: unreachable.

Inca: one of the individual rulers or members of the empire found in Peru before the Spanish conquest. The Inca spoke Quechua, a language used today by millions of Peruvians.

Incan: relating to the Inca people.

kero: a wooden goblet used by the Inca for drinking *chicha* (maize beer) during special rituals or celebrations.

llamas: domesticated South American pack animals that are also raised for their wool. Llamas are related to camels and alpacas.

maize: the Indian term for corn.

Nazca: peoples that lived on the western coast of South America in the first centuries A.D., who created the enormous, mysterious "Nazca lines," or drawings of animals or figures that are visible only from above.

niche: an (usually) arched nook, or recess, in a wall in which a statue or other artwork is displayed.

oriented: arranged in a certain position.

puma: another name for a cougar, a large wild animal of the cat family whose range includes South America. The Inca considered pumas sacred.

Quechua (KEH cha wa): the Incan language still spoken by millions of Peruvians today.

quipus **(KEY pooz):** colored and knotted strings used for recording important information.

ransom: the price in money, favors, or objects demanded or paid for the release of someone who is kidnapped or something that is captured.

siege: a military operation in which a city or fortified place is surrounded to prevent anyone from entering or escaping. A seige is often used to force the captives to surrender.

solstice: the "stopping of the Sun" — the two dates each year when the Sun reaches its greatest distance north or south of the Equator, which makes it appear to stand still in the sky.

spirit: the invisible essence of a personality, often used as another word for "soul."

stonemasonry: the cutting and preparing of stone for use in building.

tambo: a wayside or resting place for weary travelers.

temple: a building used for worship.

textile: a piece of woven or knitted cloth.

thatched: made of plant material, such as straw or palm fronds, and woven together for shelter.

tocapus: miniature boxed-in designs used in Incan weaving for telling stories or relaying messages.

Torreon: a semicircular (curved) granite altar used for solar worship at Machu Picchu. It includes a window oriented to the solstice sunrises, so that the Sun's rays shine through the opening on the biannual solstices.

trepanation: an operation during which a circular hole is cut into a living person's skull, in hope of relieving pressure on the brain.

tunic: a simple, hip-length garment with or without sleeves that slips over the head and is often worn belted.

vulnerable: capable of being physcially or psychologically harmed in some way; easy to attack.

yuca: a root vegetable, also called cassava.

MORE INFORMATION

BOOKS

The Encyclopedia of the Ancient Americas: Step into the World of the Inuit, Native American, Aztec, Maya, and Inca Peoples. Jen Green, ed. (Southwater)

Inca Life. Early Civilizations (series). David Drew (Barrons Juvenile)

Inca Town. Fiona Macdonald (Scholastic)

Incas. Ancient Civilizations (series). Duncan Scheff (Raintree Steck-Vaughn)

Lost Treasure of the Inca. Peter Lourie (Boyds Mills)

Machu Picchu: The Story of the Amazing Inkas and Their City in the Clouds. Wonders of the World (series). Elizabeth Mann (Mikaya Press)

Peru. A True Book (series). Elaine Landau (Children's Press)

WEB SITES

www.carmensandiego.com/products/time/incasc09/ebmain_c09.html
Carmen Sandiego provides five links to Incan information.

www.kent.wednet.edu/KSD/SB/Ancient/Inca.html
Elementary students report on the Inca.

www.nationalgeograhic.com/bureau/html/login.html
Discover who is buried in this tomb.

www.raingod.com/angus/Gallery/Photos/SouthAmerica/Peru/IncaTrail/index.html
Follow a virtual Inca trail to Machu Picchu.

VIDEOS

Ancient Inca. (Schlessinger)

Inca: Secrets of the Ancestors. (Time-Life)

INDEX